Who Is Vera Wang?

by Vivian Jun Kirklin

illustrated by Andrew Thomson

Penguin Workshop

For Lucy, an inspiring woman!—VJK

For Rhia, Cerys, and Esme—AT

PENGUIN WORKSHOP
An imprint of Penguin Random House LLC
1745 Broadway, New York, NY 10019
penguinrandomhouse.com

Library of Congress Cataloging-in-Publication Data is available.

First published in the United States of America by Penguin Workshop, 2026

Manufactured in the United States of America
CJKW

ISBN 9780593891445 (paperback)
10 9 8 7 6 5 4 3 2 1

ISBN 9780593891452 (library binding)
10 9 8 7 6 5 4 3 2 1

The authorized representative in the EU for product safety and compliance is Penguin Random House Ireland, Morrison Chambers, 32 Nassau Street, Dublin D02 YH68, Ireland, https://eu-contact.penguin.ie.

Contents

Who Is Vera Wang?

On June 3, 2013, Vera Wang walked into Lincoln Center in New York City to be celebrated for her impact on the fashion industry. *Fashion* is a word that refers to the types of clothing that are popular at any given moment, and fashion designers create those outfits and pieces.

After more than forty years of working in the field, Vera was being honored with a lifetime achievement award by the Council of Fashion Designers of America. The council is made up of a group of people who have dedicated their lives to celebrating and uplifting American designers who have created the best pieces of clothing.

The annual Council of Fashion Designers of America Awards are the biggest and most important honors given to fashion designers each year. Vera had already won the Womenswear Designer of the Year award in 2005. This time, she was being recognized not just for her designs but also for her lifetime of impact on the fashion world.

After important guests and fellow designers had filed into the theater, Vera's former boss and mentor, Ralph Lauren, gave a heartfelt speech that brought tears to her eyes. Then he presented her with the award.

Though Vera was a leader at the Council of Fashion Designers of America, she had been surprised and honored when she found out she was receiving the Lifetime Achievement Award. Holding the trophy, she thanked not just the people she worked with in fashion but also the people who had bought and worn her clothing over the years. She herself wore a long black silky gown from her own Vera Wang collection—with a pair of pants under it. Her outfit reflected one of her main goals as a designer: to make fashion unexpected and unique.

Following the awards ceremony, Vera hosted an after-party at the Four Seasons Restaurant. At the elegant event, famous designers mingled with Hollywood stars. Everyone was there to celebrate and honor the woman who had dressed countless celebrities on the red carpet and revolutionized the bridal gown business.

Reflecting on her success, Vera said, "I was always taught that anyone should be able to pursue their dream and that the biggest crime is not to try." Even though she had experienced moments of doubt and struggle, she said she still "would have done anything to be in fashion." With her excellent eye for style, a strong work ethic, and business smarts, her dream of working in fashion had come true in a big way.

CHAPTER 1
Fashionable Beginnings

Vera Ellen Wang was born on June 27, 1949, in New York City. Her father, Cheng Ching Wang, and her mother, Florence Wu, were born in China.

Florence Wu and Cheng Ching Wang

They both came from wealthy and prominent political families. They married in 1942, but in 1947, they fled the country. The Communist Party had overthrown the government, and civil war and unrest had made life dangerous. In order to escape the violence, they were forced to move.

Cheng Ching and Florence settled in New York City, in a neighborhood called the Upper East Side. With a master's degree in chemical engineering, Vera's father was the cofounder of a successful business called the U.S. Summit Company. Vera's mother had gone to college at a time in China when it was very rare for girls to get much of an education and even more unusual for a woman to get a college degree. Once in New York, Florence worked at the United Nations as a translator. The United Nations is an international organization focused on peace and human rights. Representatives from all over the world gather at the New York City headquarters, and translators are needed to interpret what everyone is saying.

The United Nations headquarters, New York City

Two years after Vera was born, Cheng Ching and Florence had a second child, Kenneth. Vera lived with her parents and brother in an apartment on Park Avenue filled with fine art. They spoke both English and Mandarin at home.

Kenneth and Vera

The family liked to visit museums, and they often traveled to Paris and other parts of Europe. Instead of taking a plane, they would sail on a luxury ship, the *Queen Mary*.

Vera's mother loved shopping for the newest clothing and accessories. Florence would take Vera shopping with her at high-end designer stores in New York. They would also go to Paris together to attend the shows of designers like Hubert de Givenchy and Christian Dior.

Florence was a very fashionable woman. She had a huge collection of clothes and a strong sense of style. She often ordered custom-made items from designer shops. As a result, Vera learned to appreciate fashion and design. She memorized the names of all the important designers and their styles. This exposure to art and fashion early in her childhood would set the foundation for a lifelong interest in creativity.

Fashion Shows

Fashion shows are a way for designers to display what clothes they will have for sale next season. Buyers for clothing stores, fashion journalists, celebrities, and—in recent years—social media influencers all attend to see what new styles will be available. Usually, models wear samples of the new styles and walk down a long walkway, called a runway, with the audience seated on either side. These days, though, the format of fashion shows can be very creative. They might be held outdoors, such as in a garden or city square, or in a historical building, such as a castle. In 2007, the designer house Fendi even held a fashion show on the Great Wall of China!

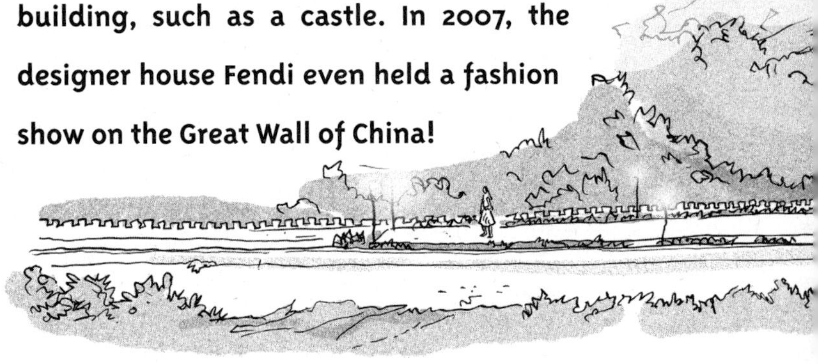

2

CHAPTER 2
School and Skating

Vera's parents placed a lot of emphasis on getting a good education. They wanted their children to be just as successful as they were. Even though the family was well off, they stressed the importance of hard work to their children. Vera attended the Chapin School from elementary school through high school. The Chapin School is a prestigious and competitive all-girls school on the Upper East Side whose former students include Jacqueline Bouvier (who would go on to be First Lady to President John F. Kennedy) and the Golden Globe–winning actress Sigourney Weaver. The classes were very demanding and challenging, so Vera had to work hard to do well.

The Chapin School

In addition to school, Vera enjoyed participating in extracurricular activities. She took lessons in ballet, tennis, and piano. Ballet was an early favorite, and she took classes at the School of American Ballet in New York.

Vera received her first pair of ice skates when she was seven years old. By the time she was ten, she was passionate about figure skating and was becoming very good at it. She began to win figure skating competitions. Early in the mornings before school, she worked with her coach, Sonya Klopfer Dunfield, at the Skating Club of New York.

Sonya Klopfer Dunfield

Vera dreamed of being in the Olympics one day. She enjoyed all parts of the sport, from the competition to the music to the costumes. In her spare time, she combined her interest in fashion with skating and sketched out ideas for figure skating costumes.

Vera began to compete as a skating pair with a partner, James Stuart. They were so good that they hoped to compete in the 1968 Winter Olympics. In order to concentrate fully on making the Olympic team, Vera took a break from school during her junior year.

Vera and James competed in the 1968 US National Championships in Philadelphia. When they did not place in the top three, they were disqualified from the Olympics. Vera was devastated. The duo competed at the national championships again the next year and won fifth place. At that time, James decided he wanted to skate solo. Vera had devoted much of her time up until then to skating. But now, nineteen years old and without a skating partner, she decided it was time to go to college and find a new dream.

Pairs Figure Skating

Olympic figure skating is divided into the men's, women's, and pairs categories. In the men's and women's categories, skaters compete solo. In pairs skating, a man and a woman skate and compete together. The two skaters must create a routine that combines elements like lifts, jumps, and spins while performing to music. Some of these elements are done side by side, at the same time. Other times, the partners may skate using different moves that are in harmony with each other. They can lose points for errors such as falling or being out of sync. The lifts, throws, spins, and jumps of pairs skating make it a risky sport! Each member of the duo must have great trust in the other in order for the pair to skate confidently.

CHAPTER 3
A Time for Transitions

In 1967, Vera had begun attending Sarah Lawrence College while she was still training to be an Olympic skater. While she still loved creating art and fashion, her father wanted her to study a subject that seemed more serious and had a more secure future, like law, business,

Sarah Lawrence College

or medicine. Vera started out as a premed student, taking classes that would be required for entering medical school.

Balancing school and skating was challenging for Vera. She had begun to feel exhausted. After James had decided to compete as a solo skater, Vera made the difficult decision to give up on her Olympic dreams.

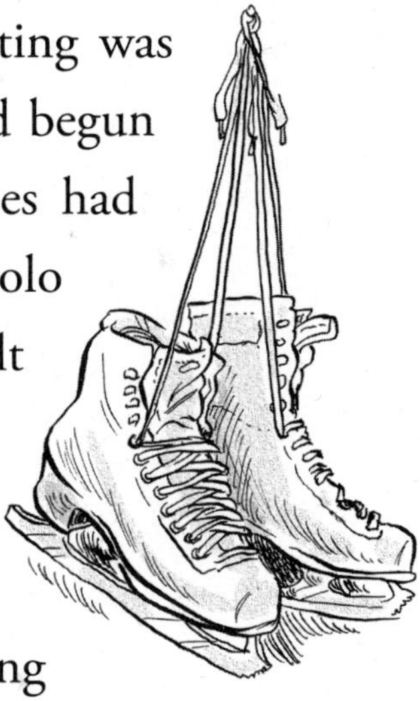

Vera also enjoyed theater and thought about becoming an actress. However, she soon realized that acting parts for Chinese American women were very limited, especially in the early 1970s when she was attending college. That was another dream that seemed unattainable.

Vera felt that she needed a change. Her premed classes were very demanding, and they did not inspire her the way the arts did. To her parents' shock, she dropped out of Sarah Lawrence during her second year and moved to Paris. She began taking classes at the Sorbonne University. There, she studied art history and found herself deeply

inspired by the historic and beautiful city around her. The art, architecture, and culture of Paris helped her realize that art history was what she wanted to continue studying.

Sorbonne University

Paris, the Fashion Capital of the World

Paris has been an important center of fashion innovation for over 350 years. During the time of King Louis XIV, nobles at his castle at Versailles (say: ver-sigh) wore fashions that were designed, made, and sold in nearby Paris. In fact, clothing from Paris was worn in royal courts all over Europe. Today, many people consider the city to be the fashion capital of the world. It is where famous designers such as Christian Dior and Coco Chanel did their work and is especially known for its high fashion, which means finely crafted and intricate clothing that is more a piece of art than just an outfit. Not only designers but also many skilled artisans who craft high fashion are located in Paris. For these reasons, today, many of the best designers around the world choose Paris as the setting for their biggest fashion shows and stores.

After months in Paris, Vera returned to New York and reentered Sarah Lawrence College as an art history major. She loved Paris so much, however, that she went back there to study abroad during her junior year, too.

On her summers off from college, Vera had her first experience working in fashion as a salesperson at the Yves Saint Laurent boutique in New York City. There, she helped customers and also worked on setting up the window displays. One summer, Vera met someone who would be very important to her career. Frances Patiky Stein was a regular customer at the boutique and an editor at *Vogue*, the most influential fashion magazine, according to many individuals in the industry. Editors at fashion

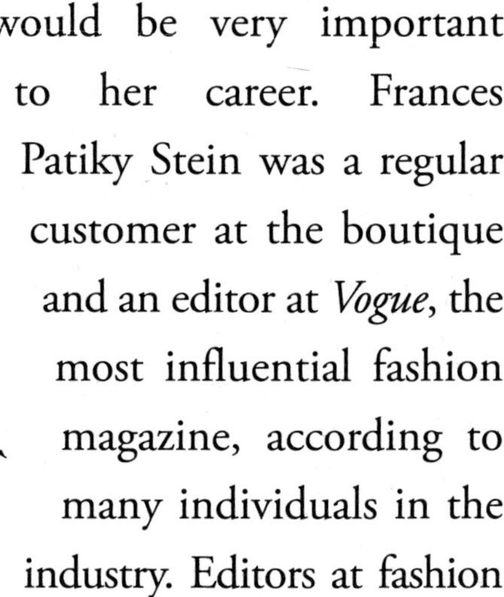

Francis Patiky Stein

magazines wrote articles, selected which styles to showcase, organized photo shoots, and more. They were often responsible for determining which trends became popular. Vera had impressed this particular editor.

CHAPTER 4
A Dream Job at *Vogue*

After graduating from Sarah Lawrence College with a degree in art history at the age of twenty-two, Vera thought about what to do next. What she really wanted to do was go to fashion school in order to become a fashion designer. However, when she shared this idea with her father, he felt it was not a good idea. He wanted her to go to law school or business school instead. Vera was not interested in either of these paths. So her father said that she should at least get a job in fashion first. That way she could figure out if becoming a designer was what she really wanted and if it was something she could succeed at.

Vera took this advice. She remembered Frances Patiky Stein, the *Vogue* editor. When Frances visited the Yves Saint Laurent store, she saw that Vera was hardworking and smart, and that she had a great sense for fashion. Frances was so impressed that she told Vera to call her if she wanted a job after graduation.

Vera made the call, and to her delight, Frances helped her get a position as an editorial assistant at *Vogue*. This job was the first step on the ladder of working at a fashion magazine. In this role, Vera would assist the editors in all kinds of ways, from making copies to helping with photo shoots.

Excited to finally be starting her career in the world of fashion, Vera showed up for her first day at *Vogue* in an elegant white Yves Saint Laurent dress and high-heeled shoes. She wanted to be prepared for this high-fashion environment. Her boss, Polly Allen Mellen, a legendary fashion editor, took one look at her and told her to go home and change. She said that they would be digging through closets full of clothes and getting dirty, so Vera's outfit would not be practical. As soon as Vera returned in more casual clothes, she dove right into the work at *Vogue*.

Polly Allen Mellen styling a model for a photo shoot

Working at *Vogue* was like a dream for Vera. She was surrounded by amazing clothes, famous designers, and the editors who would decide what would be in fashion. The job could be grueling, though. She assisted with equipment and props for photo shoots, which could happen outdoors in all kinds of weather. She swept the floors after models got haircuts. She packed and moved clothes. Even so, she was thrilled to be in the world of fashion and to be learning so much.

Polly Allen Mellen was a great mentor to her. Mentors—trusted people who teach and coach others who are less experienced in a subject—

are very valuable in a competitive industry like fashion. Polly was impressed by Vera's hardworking attitude and enthusiasm. And Vera seemed to have an instinct for fashion. She knew how to combine clothes so that even a white T-shirt could be fresh and unexpected.

It took only one year for Vera to be promoted to fashion editor. This made her, at twenty-three, one of the youngest editors in the magazine's history. Soon Vera was promoted again—to senior editor. This role launched her into another level of the fashion universe. She reviewed the clothing collections of young, new designers. Then she would select which clothes to feature in photo shoots, set up the photo shoots, and travel to oversee them. She got to know many famous designers personally and went all around the world, but she also worked late hours and was hardly ever at home from September through April, the busiest period for the magazine.

Vera had risen quickly to a high position at *Vogue*. However, after several years as a senior editor, she began to think her career might have stalled. She wanted the top job there—editor in chief. But another editor, Anna Wintour, had been working at American *Vogue* and British *Vogue*, and she was probably going to claim that post. Anna did get the job in 1988, and she revolutionized the way *Vogue* presented fashion on its pages. She realized that everyday women wanted to see styles that they could afford to buy, and so she combined high-fashion items with less expensive pieces, such as jeans. The photo shoots under her direction were also more casual and natural-looking than before.

Anna Wintour

Vera had invested fifteen years of her life in building a career at *Vogue*, only to discover that she was never going to earn the top spot at the company. Feeling disappointed, she transferred to Paris and worked as the European editor for American *Vogue*. In her new role, she spent most of her time meeting with fashion people and going to events. Although the position was a step up, she missed the hands-on aspects of working at a fashion magazine. She loved the photo shoots, selecting clothing, and styling the models.

Vera decided to leave Paris and come back to *Vogue*'s New York office. Then, after her sixteenth year at what had once felt like a dream job, she decided to finally pursue the idea that her dad had talked her out of all those years ago: becoming a designer.

Vera's Personal Style

Even though Vera would go on to design some of the dreamiest gowns for brides and Hollywood celebrities, she says she is not much of a dress girl at heart! Much of the clothing she wears is in simple colors like black, gray, and navy blue. In her everyday life, she dresses to be comfortable, in black leggings and T-shirts, and sometimes a knit hat to stay warm. But when she goes to an event or party, she brings out the fun. During her days working at *Vogue*, she would go dancing at Studio 54, a famous nightclub in New York City. She wore colorful outfits such as striped leggings with a furry coat, topped with fun, inexpensive accessories. Today, even if she is wearing just black and white, she might experiment with a bold shape or an unexpected combination, like a white floor-length gown with a hood. Even in her personal closet she selects pieces that are surprising and bold.

CHAPTER 5
Designing at Ralph Lauren

After Vera left *Vogue*, she again talked to her father about starting a design business. This time, she wanted to open her own store, and to do so, she would need financial help from him. However, her father said no. So Vera decided to work for another designer's company.

Vera got an offer to work for Geoffrey Beene, a designer who she respected very much. She knew that they had a similar drive to get all the details right on a piece of clothing. However, just as she was supposed to start, she received another job offer, this time from the designer Ralph Lauren.

Geoffrey Beene

The salary was much higher than what she would make with Geoffrey Beene. Though she hated to reject a job at the last minute, she could not turn down the higher salary. It would help her build financial independence and work toward the goal of opening her own store.

Vera began working for Ralph Lauren as a design director in 1987. In this position, she was in charge of design for accessories such as hats, belts, scarves, and jewelry. She also had a chance to design sportswear, which she loved doing.

Sportswear is the fashion term for casual clothing that might be used for athletic activities or just everyday wear. Ralph was another great mentor, and working for him gave Vera an education in the business side of designing and all the steps to making a sketch on a page become a finished piece of clothing ready to be sold.

While she was working at Ralph Lauren, Vera found more time for her personal life. She had been dating a man named Arthur Becker on and off for years. He was a businessman who she first met at a tennis match.

Back when Arthur and Vera went on their first date, Vera chose the restaurant. Arthur arrived, and he got a big surprise. Not only was Vera there, but her whole family was, too.

Arthur Becker

Arthur realized then how important family was to Vera. Her inviting them was a sign that she felt serious about beginning their relationship.

After many years of seeing each other, Arthur asked Vera to marry him. At a dinner with their close friends, Arthur hid an engagement ring in a piece of cake. Vera started eating the cake but luckily didn't eat the ring! When she spotted it, she realized what was happening. She said yes to marrying Arthur. The wedding date was set for June 1989, just before Vera's fortieth birthday.

Once the date for the wedding was set, Vera began one of the most important tasks: selecting her wedding gown. She went to stores all over New York for months but didn't find anything that she liked. As a designer and a former *Vogue* editor, Vera was, of course, very choosy. But she truly felt that the wedding dresses she had found didn't quite match her style. The gowns that were popular in those days were frilly and over-the-top, with full skirts, puff sleeves, and bows.

As a high-powered woman who worked in fashion and preferred to dress elegantly, Vera could not see herself wearing one of these dresses.

Vera decided that if she wanted a wedding dress that reflected her style, she had to design it herself. She sketched out her ideas, finalized the design, and hired a tailor to make it. On her wedding day, June 22, 1989, Vera wore her creation.

It was a white satin gown with a clean, simple shape and beads sewn all over. Later on, during the reception, she changed into a different dress, following the Chinese tradition of the bride wearing multiple outfits during the wedding day.

This dress was a light, sleek pink one that was a little more comfortable than her heavier wedding dress.

Vera's difficult experience trying to find a dress for her wedding would stick with her. Not only was buying her own dress a challenge, but finding dresses that suited her bridesmaids was challenging, too. Her friends, who were a lot like

1980s bridesmaids dresses

herself, had said that they felt like backup singers in a band when they were wearing the matching bridesmaids' dresses. As Vera began to consider her next move in the fashion industry, these frustrating experiences would turn into great inspiration.

Ralph Lauren (1939–)

In the world of American fashion, Ralph Lauren is considered a pioneer. He started out designing and selling men's ties in 1967. A few years later, he began designing women's clothing, too, and then launched his version of the polo shirt. This short-sleeve pullover cotton shirt with a collar and polo player logo came in many colors and was hugely popular. Ralph's designs focused less on trends and more on timeless style. They were seen as easy and classic. Today, the Ralph Lauren company still makes full lines of clothing for men and women, along with many other products, such as children's clothing, bedding and towels, fragrances, and eyewear. It operates hundreds of stores in dozens of countries around the world. In 2025, Ralph Lauren even became the first fashion designer ever to receive the Presidential Medal of Freedom.

CHAPTER 6
Vera Wang Bridal

After Vera and Arthur's wedding, they wanted to start a family right away. However, when Vera had difficulty becoming pregnant, she decided to take a break from work. The constant doctor's appointments and hospital visits were too much when combined with her demanding job. She left the Ralph Lauren company in 1989, having worked there for two years.

Vera soon found out from her doctors that she was unable to get pregnant. She felt extremely sad about it. Though she was disappointed, she kept moving forward. At this time, she began thinking about what her next step would be in her fashion career. Calvin Klein, a very famous designer, offered her a job working for him. But what Vera really wanted to do was finally start her own design business.

Calvin Klein

Having watched Vera create her own wedding gown, her father had seen that there were too few elegant, high-fashion styles available in bridal stores and that Vera had a talent for designing them. He offered to give her the money to help start her own bridal business.

At first, Vera was unsure she wanted to do this. She had never imagined herself being a bridal designer. At the time, this was not something that serious fashion designers did. But she soon began to see that there was a real opportunity to bring fashion to the bridal industry. She had experienced what it was like to go shopping for a wedding gown and only find old-fashioned and traditional dresses.

She took her father up on his offer. With a loan from him, she rented a store in the Carlyle Hotel in Manhattan.

Then she brought on Chet Hazzard, a good friend in the fashion industry, to help her plan and manage it.

Vera got to work fixing up and redesigning the two-story shop. She wanted it to feel elegant and high-end. Vera Wang Bridal House, as it was officially known, opened in September 1990.

Chet Hazzard

At first, she sold expensive, high-quality bridal gowns by other designers. It was a tough time to open a store, because the US economy was not doing very well. She had some help from her former coworkers in the fashion world, though. *Vogue* ran a six-page article all about her luxurious new business, which was great publicity.

Around that time, Vera's dream of starting a family came true. She and Arthur adopted a baby girl shortly after her birth in 1990, naming her Cecilia.

In the meantime, Vera Wang Bridal House was becoming a full-service bridal shop. The store not only provided gowns for brides but also helped them with many of the other details of a wedding, like how the brides could style their hair, what jewelry to wear, and what flowers to carry.

About two years after opening the store, Vera began to design her own wedding gowns. At first, it was hard to find the time—she was running the store and raising her daughter. She would sketch designs whenever she could, sometimes while watching TV in the evenings at home.

Vera's designs were clean and modern but with a focus on luxurious details. They were made of fine fabrics like silk and featured beading and sheer sections. Vera wanted to use only the highest-quality fabrics on her gowns, and when she couldn't find materials that matched her standards, she and Chet built factories that would make them. She was very focused on fit, making sure that her designs looked good on women of all body types. Vera's goal was to make any woman feel confident and comfortable. She also innovated with color, adding small pops of color on traditionally white or cream gowns, or even offering wedding gowns in solid colors other than white.

The History of Wedding Dresses

Today, wedding dresses are usually white or off-white. But before the 1900s, white was not always the color brides wore. In fact, fashion historians say that it was after Queen Victoria of England wore a white wedding gown in 1840 that the color became popular.

Wearing a dress specifically made for your wedding dates back to ancient China. Chinese legends depict brides wearing red, which is a color that is connected with good luck in the culture. Today, many Chinese brides still choose red for their wedding dresses.

Red is also considered a lucky color in India, where many brides wear a red-and-gold lehenga (say: luh-heng-a). A lehenga is a bridal outfit made up of a skirt, a fitted cropped shirt, and a veil.

Queen Victoria

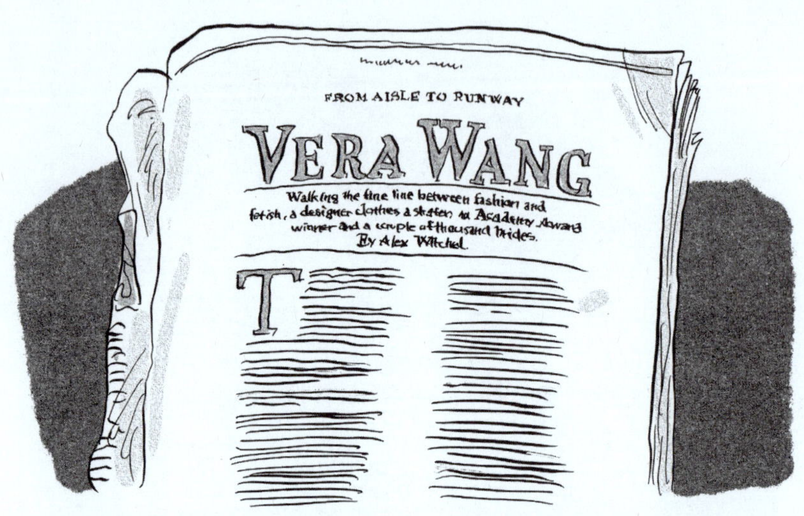

Vera's wedding gown designs received glowing reviews in major publications such as the *New York Times*. Word spread, and Vera Wang became one of the most coveted brands for designer wedding gowns. Soon, she sold her gowns not only at her own store but at luxury department stores as well. She began to design bridesmaids' dresses and nonbridal evening gowns as well. Then Vera's success gave her the opportunity to return to one of her old passions—figure skating.

CHAPTER 7
Mixing Fashion with Skating

When Vera gave up her dreams of a figure skating career back in college, little did she know that she would return to the sport in another way. Vera had already made a name for herself as a bridal designer when she was asked to design a figure skating costume for Nancy Kerrigan. Nancy Kerrigan was a rising skater who had won the bronze medal at the 1991 World Figure Skating Championships and qualified for the 1992 Winter Olympics. Her coach, whom Vera

Nancy Kerrigan

knew from her own figure skating days, asked if Vera would be interested in designing Nancy's costume.

At first, Vera was unsure. This was no simple request. The costume not only had to be beautiful but also had to withstand the highly athletic moves of a skater. As Vera said, "If one strap were to break, or if the beading on the sleeve gets caught when they turn, their whole Olympics is over." The extreme speed and positions a skater's body takes during competition mean costumes have to be incredibly flexible, light, and durable. One wrong stitch could lead to a costume disaster that ends a performance. But even though she felt nervous, Vera was not one to back down from a challenge.

Vera agreed to design a costume for Nancy, and what she came up with was unlike anything the other skaters were wearing. At the time, figure skating costumes for women were often covered with sequins and ruffles. Vera's design was all white, with a clean, simple silhouette. It displayed her signature craftsmanship. The chest featured woven detailing, and the neckline and arms were made of sheer, stretchy fabric. The collar was decorated with rhinestones that gave it the look of a diamond necklace.

Figure Skating Jumps

The main types of jumps that are performed in competitive figure skating are the loop, the Salchow (say: sal-cow), the axel, the toe loop, the lutz, and the flip. The differences between the jumps are whether the skater takes off from the toe of the skate or the edge, whether the jump is done forward or backward, and what leg the skater lands on. Each of these jumps can be done as a single, double, triple, or quadruple—which is determined by how many times the skater rotates in the air before landing. Of course, the higher the number, the more difficult the jump is! Skaters are judged on factors like how high their jumps are, how effortless they appear, whether the jumps happen in rhythm, and how cleanly the takeoffs and landings go.

Skater Mirai Nagasu performs a triple axel

The costume was similar to Vera's wedding dresses, but it was also specifically designed with Nancy in mind. Vera wanted to create something that would match the skater's elegant, sophisticated look. The result was such a success that other skaters began to ask her to design for them.

Because Vera herself had been a figure skater competing at a high level, she had special knowledge about how the costume should move and feel. Her perspective as a former athlete combined with her artistic talent made her a groundbreaking designer in the figure skating world.

CHAPTER 8
Red Carpets and Runways

In 1993, Vera's business was soaring. Her wedding dress designs were setting the standard

for luxury bridal fashion. But Vera had her sights set on even bigger stages.

Vera's years at *Vogue* and working for Ralph Lauren had taught her that in order to be a successful designer, her clothes had to be seen by the biggest possible audience. Even if she created the most beautiful and well-made dresses,

if no one knew about them, no one would buy them. But for the first few years she was in business, she didn't hold fashion shows because they were so expensive to put on. Instead, she kept an eye out for celebrities who would wear her designs.

Through a friend, Vera met Sharon Stone, who was an up-and-coming actress.

Sharon Stone

When Sharon was invited to the 1993 Academy Awards, also known as the Oscars, she agreed to let Vera design her outfit. The dress that Vera came up with was a blond-colored satin ball gown with a matching belt. Sharon's look on the Oscars red carpet that year stood out. At the time, people had been dressing more casually at the Oscars. Vera's design helped bring more glamorous outfits back to the event.

Although Sharon Stone's 1993 Oscars dress was Vera's first red-carpet moment, it certainly wouldn't be her last. Her dresses became highly in demand for the Oscars and other major events.

Not only was Vera's business growing, but her family was growing, too. Vera and Arthur were thrilled when they were able to adopt a second daughter, Josephine, soon after her birth in 1993. Now with two daughters, who she called Cesi and Jojo, Vera was busier than ever.

All the celebrities wearing Vera's designs made them even more popular. In April 1998, she held her first official runway show in New York City.

A fashion show was a huge event. Fashion editors, journalists, photographers, and celebrities would all be attending to get the first peek at Vera's eveningwear offerings for the upcoming season. Models walked down the runway wearing her newest designs. Journalists and editors loved the collection, and the show was a big success.

Fashion Week

Fashion Week is a time when designers present their new collections of clothing at runway shows. This weeklong event happens twice a year, in February and September. In February, designs for the upcoming fall and winter are presented, and in September, designs for the next spring and summer are presented.

A typical runway show at Fashion Week is only ten to twenty minutes long, and there are usually dozens of shows during the week. With so many happening at once, designers try to make their collections stand out. They might show bold and unusual looks that aren't really meant to be sold in stores. Even if a person wouldn't buy these designs for everyday wear, they represent the artistic vision of the designer and inspire the next season's fashion trends. New York Fashion Week is usually the first of the season, and other cities, including London, Milan, and Paris, hold their own fashion weeks shortly after.

Hillary Clinton in a Vera Wang gown

Vera's designs had become so famous that important people in politics wore her dresses as well. In 1997, when President Bill Clinton and First Lady Hillary Clinton welcomed the Chinese president Jiang Zemin to a state dinner at the White House, Hillary wore a Vera Wang gown. Vera was even a guest at the dinner.

CHAPTER 9
Expanding Her Empire

In 2000, Vera expanded her line further into ready-to-wear, or premade clothing that is sold in set sizes. Previously, most of Vera's designs had to be specially ordered and fitted to each customer. Now people could try on and buy her clothes right off the rack. Her first collection featured modern-looking dresses that were for more casual occasions.

Another exciting opportunity came along for Vera in 2000. In this year, she made a deal with a cosmetics company to create her own perfume. Her fragrance, simply called Vera Wang, went on sale in 2002.

Vera became a book author in 2001 when she published *Vera Wang on Weddings*. It gave brides-to-be ideas and advice on everything from wedding gowns to wedding cakes. The pages were filled with

photos from real-life weddings, and many of the brides shown were celebrities. The book also included illustrated examples of all the parts of a wedding dress and how they could be styled differently.

Vera's collaborations continued to grow. She designed a collection of eyeglasses in 2001. Then, in 2002, she designed home products, including fine dishes and vases, for Wedgwood. The famous chinaware company had been around since 1759, and it was the first time in their long history that they had ever done a designer collaboration. Vera also designed shoes that would pair well with her wedding and evening gowns. She worked with the shoe companies Stuart Weitzman and Giuseppe Zanotti to create them. During this time, Vera's wedding gown business was still thriving. In 2001 alone, Vera Wang Bridal sold more than ten thousand gowns.

In January 2004, Vera's mother, Florence, passed away. Her stylish mother had been her original inspiration for entering the world of fashion. She had introduced a young Vera to fashion shows and high-end designers. Vera had dedicated her book on weddings to Florence. The loss was a very difficult one.

Then in March 2005, Chet Hazzard, Vera's business partner, died. He had been with her from the very beginning of Vera Wang Bridal. She was heartbroken to lose him.

Through these difficult times, Vera kept working. Her ready-to-wear collections now included a full range of pieces, like shirts, pants, and skirts, and could be bought at major department stores. They made such an impact that in 2005, she received the award for Womenswear Designer of the Year from the Council of Fashion Designers of America. She described getting this award as a lifelong dream come true.

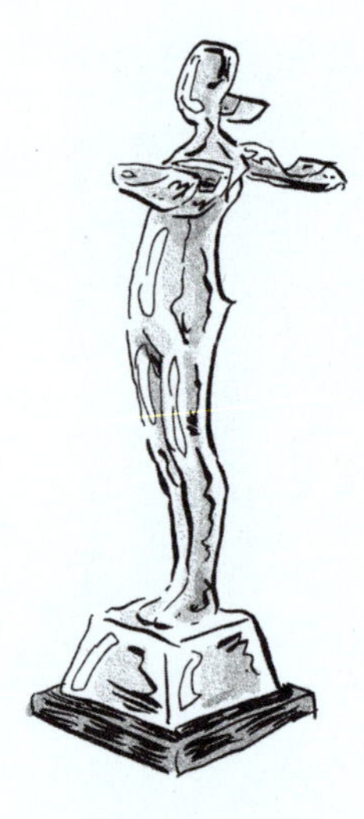

Vera experienced another major loss in 2006. Right before one of her fashion shows, her father died. Vera's father had always been one of her toughest critics but also one of her biggest supporters. He had been the first to suggest that she go into the bridal business. After being at her father's bedside when he died, she had to leave to present her show. At the end of the show, she greeted her audience with tears on her face.

Even though she was now making clothes sold in department stores where anyone could shop, actresses who wanted to make a memorable impression on the red carpet came to Vera. Famous brides who were looking for the most stylish, luxurious, and even comfortable wedding dresses came to Vera.

While Vera had fun designing glamorous gowns for major celebrities, she wanted her clothes to be worn by even more people. So she next turned her thoughts to designing a line of affordable clothing. In 2007, she collaborated with Kohl's to create the Simply Vera line, which featured casual items that could be mixed and matched.

Simply Vera clothing

As she built her fashion empire, Vera continued to design for figure skaters. After years of designing these costumes, she was given an incredible honor. Her contributions to figure skating fashion were so significant that in 2009, she was inducted into the US Figure Skating Hall of Fame. Vera had dreamed of being an Olympic skater herself, but her impact as a designer on the figure skating world was just as monumental.

She designed her first figure skating costume for a man when she created Evan Lysacek's costume in 2010. The requirements were somewhat different. As always, the costume had to feel light and flexible during the frequent jumps he would be doing, but all the seams were quadruple stitched because of how much force Evan generated on his spins. In the end, she designed an all-black costume with leather and sequin details that he wore during his gold-medal performance.

Evan Lysacek at the 2010 Winter Olympics

Many brides dreamed of getting married in one of Vera's dresses, but most people could not afford a custom-made gown. In 2011, she launched a line of much more affordable designs for David's Bridal. This gave more brides everywhere the chance to wear a Vera Wang gown on their wedding day.

Vera Wang's David's Bridal collection

Though Vera was more successful than ever, she still faced hardships. In 2012, she and Arthur divorced. While this was challenging for Vera, she and Arthur remained friends and continued to raise their two daughters together.

CHAPTER 10
Still Innovating

Vera's impact on the fashion world continued to grow. First Lady Michelle Obama wore Vera Wang to a state dinner in 2015. The elegant black dress that Vera designed for her received rave reviews. Among the celebrities Vera has dressed for the red carpet are Sandra Bullock, Nicole Kidman, Oprah, Ariana Grande, Katy Perry, Selena Gomez, Constance Wu, Emma Watson, Zendaya, and Janelle Monáe.

Famous brides who have worn Vera Wang to their weddings include Chelsea Clinton, Gwen Stefani, Alicia Keys, Issa Rae, Mariah Carey, Victoria Beckham, and Jennifer Lopez. The actress Sarah Hyland wore not one but two Vera Wang gowns for her wedding.

Ariana Grande and Vera Wang

For her wedding to Justin Bieber in 2023, Hailey Bieber also wore multiple dresses. She chose a Vera Wang gown to wear in the second part of her reception. The dress was made of a light, silky satin with straps that crisscrossed in the back. It was made to be comfortable for dancing, and Hailey paired it with shoes that she could dance in as well—white sneakers!

Hailey Bieber

Nathan Chen

Vera continued to design stunning figure skating costumes, including ones for world champion Nathan Chen. Considered one of the greatest men's figure skaters of all time, he is known for his quadruple jumps, which are so difficult that very few skaters can even perform them. Vera designed his costumes for the 2022 Olympics, where he won his first Olympic gold medals.

Over the course of her career, Vera has had the chance to design multiple Barbie dolls. In 1998, her first Barbie came out, dressed in a white satin bridal gown with black velvet details. She also designed a Barbie wearing a purple evening gown in 1999. But the most important Barbie that she worked on came in 2022 when Vera herself was honored in Mattel's limited-edition Barbie Tribute Collection, which features people who have influenced culture in an important way.

Vera Wang Barbie doll

In her Barbie form, Vera wears an all-black outfit from one of her ready-to-wear collections.

In 2024, the actress Anna Sawai became the first Asian woman to win the Emmy Award for Lead Actress in a Drama Series. It was fitting that she wore a gown by Vera Wang, the most successful Asian American fashion designer, as she accepted her historic award.

Today, Vera has shops around the world. Cities with Vera Wang bridal stores include London, Shanghai, Tokyo, Sydney, and Seoul. She has designed clothing for movies and TV shows.

Vera continues to be in the public eye. The media pays attention to what she wears, and she makes headlines for her bold personal style. She also offers advice to young designers. Because she has experienced so many different parts of the fashion industry, she has a lot of valuable information to share.

Anna Sawai

Although Vera has faced her share of disappointments and challenges, she never gave up on her dreams. She was lucky to have grown up in one of the greatest cities in the world, with museums and designer shops so close by. However, she never took any opportunities for granted. Her parents taught her to work hard and to make smart, practical decisions. These lessons, combined with her passion for beauty and creativity, continue to drive her forward.

Timeline of Vera Wang's Life

1949	Vera Ellen Wang is born
1967	Begins attending Sarah Lawrence College
1969	Competes for the second time in the US Figure Skating Championships
1971	Graduates from Sarah Lawrence and begins work at *Vogue*
1972	Is promoted to fashion editor at *Vogue*
1987	Leaves *Vogue* and begins working at Ralph Lauren
1989	Marries Arthur Becker. Leaves position at Ralph Lauren
1990	Opens Vera Wang Bridal House
	Cecilia Becker is born and adopted by Vera and Arthur shortly after
1992	Designs her own line of wedding gowns
1993	Vera and Arthur's second adopted daughter, Josephine, is born
1998	Holds her first runway show
2001	Her book, *Vera Wang on Weddings*, is published
2005	Receives the Womenswear Designer of the Year award from the CFDA
2013	Receives the Lifetime Achievement Award from the CFDA
2022	Mattel creates a Vera Wang doll for their Barbie Tribute Collection

Timeline of the World

1949	Mao Zedong declares the start of the People's Republic of China
1954	Coco Chanel holds her first fashion show since the start of World War II
1963	The Beatles release their first record
1965	The Voting Rights Act is passed in the United States
1976	Apple Computer, Inc., is founded
1987	The world population reaches five billion
1990	The Hubble Space Telescope is launched
1991	Children's book creator Dr. Seuss passes away
1995	*Toy Story*, the first full-length computer-animated movie, debuts
1997	Netflix is launched, offering customers DVD rentals by mail
1998	Google is founded by two university students
2002	The Winter Olympics are held in Salt Lake City, Utah
2004	Facebook is launched
2009	Barack Obama becomes the first Black president of the United States
2018	Meghan Markle and Prince Harry get married
2019	The US women's soccer team sets a record with a fourth World Cup title

Bibliography

***Books for young readers**

"An After-Party in Honor of Wang's CFDA Lifetime Achievement Award." ***Vogue***. June 4, 2013. https://www.vogue.com/article/a-cfda-after-party-in-honor-of-vera-wangs-lifetime-achievement-award.

Beard, Alison. "Life's Work: An Interview with Vera Wang." ***Harvard Business Review***. July–August 2019. https://hbr.org/2019/07/lifes-work-an-interview-with-vera-wang.

"The CFDA Winners 2005." ***British Vogue***. June 7, 2005. https://www.vogue.co.uk/article/the-cfda-winners-2005.

Critchell, Samantha. "Vera Wang Honored for Her Lifetime Fashion Passion." ***Washington Post***. June 8, 2013. https://www.washingtonpost.com/lifestyle/style/vera-wang-honored-for-her-lifetime-fashion-passion/2013/06/06/32dbd932-cd2a-11e2-8845-d970ccb04497_story.html.

Fasanella, Allie. "At 28, Vera Wang Worked at *Vogue* and Partied at Studio 54." ***Bustle***. July 1, 2022. https://www.bustle.com/style/vera-wang-vogue-editor-career-studio-54-age-28-interview.

Frey, Kaitlyn. "Vera Wang Reflects on More Than 20 Years of Designing Olympic Figure Skating Costumes." ***People***. Feb. 12, 2018. https://people.com/style/vera-wang-interview-design-figure-skating-costumes/.

Givhan, Robin. "A Normal Person's Guide to Understanding a

Fashion Week Runway Show." ***Washington Post***. Feb. 7, 2018. https://www.washingtonpost.com/lifestyle/style/a-normal-persons-guide-to-understanding-a-fashion-week-runway-show/2018/02/06/582e4b94-008c-11e8-8acf-ad2991367d9d_story.html.

Goh, Z. K. "Vera Wang Talks About Her Olympics Ambitions." Olympics.com. Nov. 3, 2020. https://olympics.com/en/news/vera-wang-talks-about-her-olympics-ambitions.

Gonzalez, Sandra. "Vera Wang on Her 'Firsts.' " ***Entertainment Weekly***. May 28, 2013. https://ew.com/article/2013/05/28/designer-vera-wang-remembers-her-fashion-firsts/.

"How I Got There." ***Newsweek***. Nov. 13, 2005. https://www.newsweek.com/how-i-got-there-115587.

Lipsky-Karasz, Elisa. "The Vera Wang Interview: Made of Honor." ***Harper's Bazaar***. Mar. 24, 2011. https://www.harpersbazaar.com/fashion/designers/a694/vera-wang-interview/.

*Krohn, Katherine. ***Vera Wang: Enduring Style***. Minneapolis: Twenty-First Century Books, 2009.

Malach, Hannah. "How Vera Wang Went from Ice Skater to the A-List Crowd's Top Bridal Designer." ***Women's Wear Daily***. Nov. 3, 2023. https://wwd.com/feature/vera-wang-history-1235909839/.

Menkes, Suzy. "Taking China: Vera Wang's Long March." ***New York Times***. Jan 10. 2006. https://www.nytimes.com/2006/01/10/style/taking-china-vera-wangs-long-march.html.

Michie, Natalie. "The History of the White Shirt at the Oscars, from Sharon Stone to Zendaya." ***Fashion***. March 7, 2023. https://fashionmagazine.com/style/celebrity-style/oscars-2022-white-button-down-shirt/.

Steele, Valerie, ed. ***Paris: Capital of Fashion***. London: Bloomsbury, 2019.

Steele, Valerie. ***Paris Fashion: A Cultural History***. Oxford, UK: Berg, 1998.

*Todd, Anne M. ***Vera Wang***. New York: Chelsea House, 2007.

"Vera Wang." Biography.com. May 13, 2021. https://www.biography.com/history-culture/vera-wang.

"Vera Wang." ***Britannica***. Updated June 23, 2025. https://www.britannica.com/biography/Vera-Wang.

"Vera Wang." ***Newsmakers***. Gale, 1998. https://link.gale.com/apps/doc/K1618002608/BIC?u=indymar&sid=bookmark-BIC&xid=455b3cfb.

Vineyard, Jennifer. "Vera Wang Says: Know When to Walk Away . . . and Start Something New." The Cut. June 24, 2015. https://www.thecut.com/2015/06/vera-wang-says-know-when-to-walk-away.html.

Wang, Vera. ***Vera Wang on Weddings***. New York: HarperCollins, 2001.